Highlights

CHRISTMAS PUZZLE AND PLAY

BUILD WITH 100 PIECES!

Flip to the back for Plus-Plus instructions!

HIGHLIGHTS PRESS
Honesdale, Pennsylvania

W0013919

baseball bat

envelope

rabbit

snail

fishing pole

Christmas Preparation

magnifying glass

bat

ring

baseball

fish

The elves are getting ready for the holiday! Can you find all the hidden objects?

Art by Josh Cleland

ruler

sailboat

glo...

m...

pencil

toy top

wedge of cheese

button

Animals' Tree

The animals will love this Christmas treat! Can you find all the hidden objects?

candle

mushroom

peanut

spoon

crescent moon

ghost

chicken

slice of pizza

picture frame

feather

leaf

sock

whale

pencil

clamshell

fork

Art by Gary Mohrman

4

Post Office Presents

Art by Gary LaCoste

Six by Six

Each of these small scenes contains **6** hidden objects from the list below. Some objects are hidden in more than one scene. Can you find the **6** hidden objects in each scene?

Hidden Object List

The numbers tell you how many times each object is hidden.

bell (3)
boomerang (3)
button (4)
cane (4)
crescent moon (4)
crown (2)
fork (2)
heart (4)
ruler (3)
slice of cake (2)
tack (2)
worm (3)

BONUS
Two scenes contain the exact same set of hidden objects. Can you find that matching pair?

Penguin Songs

Sing along with the penguin choir as you find the hidden objects.

Art by Lorraine Dey

sailboat

pennant

lollipop

envelope

screwdriver

strawberry

cupcake

comb

Trim the Tree

How would you decorate your Christmas tree? Draw it here.

Art by Svetlana Larshina/GettyImages

kite

question mark

spool of thread

crescent moon

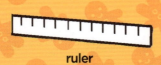
ruler

drum

crown

comb

seashell

shuttlecock

test tube

top hat

flag

paddle

feather

tube of paint

crayon

Art by Dana Regan

11

Merry Music

Can you find at least **14** differences between these two pictures?

What do alpacas sing at Christmas?

Fa-la-la-la-la, la-la-llama.

What do sheep say to shepherds at Christmastime?

Season's bleatings!

Art by Josh Cleland

What is a librarian's favorite Christmas carol?

Silent Night.

What did the beaver say to the Christmas tree?

Nice gnawing you!

Holiday Shopping

spoon

pennant

sailboat

magnet

ladle

lighthouse

magnifying glass

saucepan

horn

fishhook

skateboard

eyeglasses

lampshade

BAKERY

boomerang

closed umbrella

toothbrush

hockey stick

ice-cream bar

rocket ship

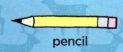
pencil

slice of pizza

shovel

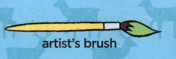
artist's brush

paint bucket

ring

Art by Kelly Kennedy

Snow Day

There are **6** words (not pictures!) hidden in this scene. Can you find BOOTS, CHILL, FROST, ICE, MITTENS, and SNOW?

Art by Kelly Kennedy

Say each tongue twister three times fast!

Silly snowmen make children smile.

No nose knows snow like a snowman's nose knows.

Shovel snow slowly.

Gingerbread House

What a festive gingerbread house! Can you find all the hidden objects?

Art by R. Michael Palan

toothbrush

ring

teacup

candle

pencil

golf club

needle

spatula

snake

nail

fishhook

wishbone

handbell

tack

spoon

Snowshoe Globes

Can you find at least **15** differences between these two pictures?

Art by Kevin Zimmer

Tic Tac Row

What do the sweaters in each row (horizontally, vertically, and diagonally) have in common?

Art by John Herzog

Who hides in the bakery at Christmas?

A mince spy.

What kind of Christmas sweater does a pirate wear?

Arrr-gyle.

Give this boy something to think. Then find the hidden cane, football, pencil, slice of pizza, and stamp.

Jingle Bell Rock

Time to make some merry music! Can you find all the hidden objects?

Art by David Helton

crown

sailboat

golf club

sock

necktie

screwdriver

chili pepper

puzzle piece

flowerpot

leaf

loaf of bread

wedge of lemon

kite

seashell

pencil

Merry Christmas

pickle

stocking

snowman

holly

peppermint

mitten

snowflake

toy bag

musical note

reindeer

sled

bell

santa hat

ice skate

This street has been decorated . . . with hidden objects!
Can you find all the objects hidden in this photo?

Christmas tree

mug

teddy bear

star

piece of candy

candle

candy cane

Art by Rich Powell

string of lights

sleigh

wreath

Christmas tree ornament

gift

gingerbread cookie

Christmas Concert

spoon

travel mug

musical note

L square

horseshoe

envelope

crown

flashlight

magnifying glass

wedge of lemon

snake

slice of pizza

bell

leaf

sock

domino

pencil

baseball

boomerang

golf club

heart

bowling ball

bowl

teacup

baseball bat

Art by Mitch Mortimer

27

Time to Party

Unwrap some gifts with these elves, then find all the hidden objects.

artist's brush
lamp
tack
hammer
beachball
domino
needle
lollipop
bird
book
candle
ladder
traffic cone
candy cane
pennant
party hat
pencil
pocket watch
slice of pie
butterfly
worm
ring
caterpillar
toothbrush
snake
heart
banana
sock
crown
snow cone
magnet
bell
leaf

Art by Diana Zourelias

Christmas Town

HOLLY'S

MAIL

Merry 4th of July

TOY

XMAS TREES

SKI 1

Art by Kelly Kennedy

How does a polar bear decorate for Christmas?

With mistle-snow.

What is another name for an artificial Christmas tree?

Faux fir.

Each of these scenes contains 12 hidden objects, which are listed below. Find each object in one of the scenes, then cross it off the list.

Art by Chuck Dillon

ball	caterpillar	horseshoe	seal
banana	chicken	megaphone	shovel
bell	envelope	mop	slice of pie
boot	fish	penguin	stocking
candle	hammer	pitcher	squeegee
canoe	hockey stick	sailboat	toothbrush

Build a sand-person, then find the hidden objects.

hourglass

ballet slipper

Christmas light bulb

crayon

pine cone

snowflake

Art by Jennifer Zivoin

boot

glove

peapod

sailboat

feather

rabbit

Can you hide this elf's hat in your own Hidden Pictures drawing?

ice-cream cone

boot

spoon

hairbrush

clothespin

nail

penguin

frog

bell

fishhook

arrow

bird

ant

roller skate

mitten

fish

strawberry

sailboat

toothbrush

key

three ducks

seal

saw

fork

shoe

Art by Valeri Gorbachev

Night Skate

There are **6** words (not pictures!) hidden in this scene. Can you find COOL, CUT, MAN, SEE, SNOW, and TELL?

Art by Jackie Stafford

Say each tongue twister three times fast!

Twila twirled twenty times.

I see icy ice skaters.

Skipper skated skillfully.

Let's Decorate

These friends are having fun decorating the tree. Can you find all the hidden objects?

MERRY CHRISTMAS

Art by Sally Springer

spoon

book

mitten

sailboat

high-heeled shoe

clothespin

envelope

hairbrush

mug

Light Show

canoe

wedge of lime

pencil

crown

slice of pizza

paintbrush

button

spool of thread

horseshoe

shark

piece of popcorn

banana

funnel

toothbrush

bell

golf club

sock

hammer

puzzle piece

envelope

Art by Dave Klug

crayon

comb

needle

carrot

ruler

41

Tic Tac Row

What do the snow globes in each row (horizontally, vertically, and diagonally) have in common?

Art by Garry Colby

Which reindeer loves to tango?

Dancer.

How does a Christmas tree keep its breath fresh?

With orna-mints.

Double Birds

Can you find at least **18** differences between these two pictures?

Art by Kevin Zimmer

How would you decorate gingerbread cookies? Decorate the cookies here.

Art by LokFung/GettyImages

Winter Journey

These animals have reached the North Pole! Can you find all the hidden objects?

Art by Mark Corcoran

tent

ax

wishbone

scissors

ice-cream cone

ghost

crown

lollipop

shoe

high-heeled shoe

tape dispenser

whale

toaster

firefighter's helmet

Ornament Match

Every ornament in the picture has one that looks just like it. Can you find all **10** matching pairs?

Snow Go!

You won't be snow "bored" if you find the clear path to the FINISH. If you run into a black line, you're going the wrong way!

START

FINISH

Candy Canes

Can you find the apple, bell, cherries, fire hydrant, heart, ice skate, lobster, magnet, mitten, mug, necktie, scarf, sled, snowflake, and strawberry?

BONUS! Find seven cardinals.

Letter Drop

Only **6** of the letters in the top line will work their way through this maze to land in the numbered squares at the bottom. When they get there, they will spell out the answer to the riddle.

A C H B E R A O R R L D E

1 2 3 4 5 6

What do you call a flamingo at the North Pole?

___ ___ ___ ___ ___ ___
1   2   3   4   5   6

Art by Jim Paillot

Night Flight

ladder

shoe

piece of popcorn

cookie

snow cone

heart

canoe

mitten

comb

needle

pencil

fishhook

Santa's on his way! Can you find all the hidden objects?

bell

envelope

balloon

magnet

ice-cream
bar

hockey
stick

crown

football

ruler

sailboat

worm

slice of pizza

golf club

Art by Gary LaCoste

51

Answers

▼ Pages 2–3

▼ Page 4

▼ Pages 6–7

▼ Page 8

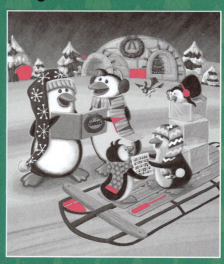

▼ Pages 10–11

▼ Pages 12–13

Answers

▼ Pages 14–15

▼ Page 16

▼ Page 17

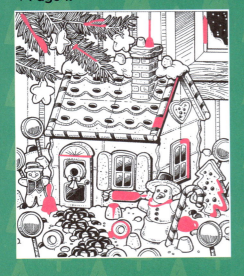

▼ Page 18

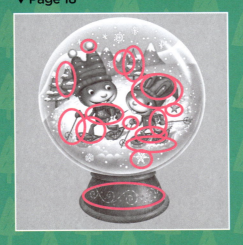

▼ Page 19

▼ Page 20

▼ Page 21

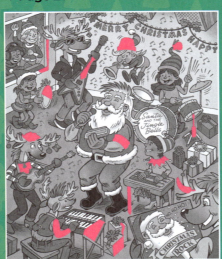

Answers

▼ Pages 22–23

▼ Pages 26–27

▼ Page 28

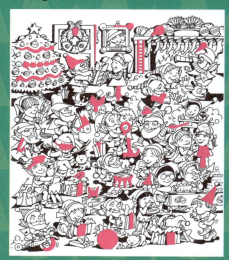

▼ Pages 30–31

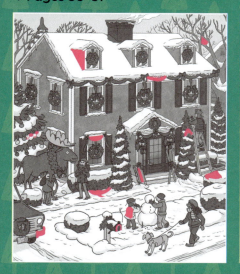

▼ Page 32

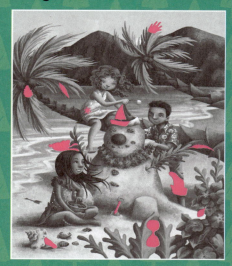

Answers

▼ Pages 34–35

▼ Page 36

▼ Page 37

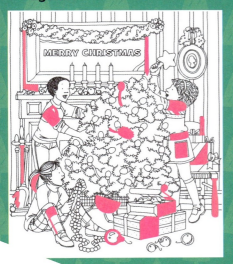

▼ Pages 38–39

▼ Page 42

Answers

▼ Page 43

▼ Page 45

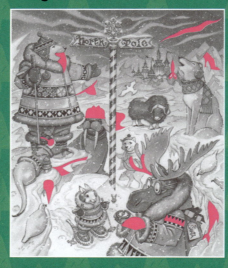

▼ Page 46

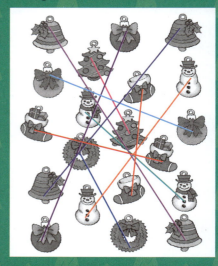

▼ Page 47

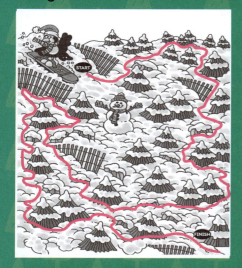

▼ Page 48

▼ Page 49

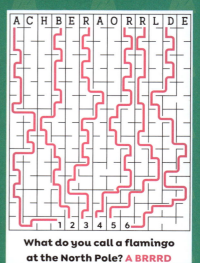

What do you call a flamingo at the North Pole? A BRRRD

▼ Pages 50–51

CHRISTMAS
PUZZLE AND PLAY
PLUS-PLUS
INSTRUCTIONS

Or anything you can imagine!

TRIM the TREE

1   2 ✛

2   2 ✛

3   2 ✛

4   5 ✛

5   1 ✛   6 ✛

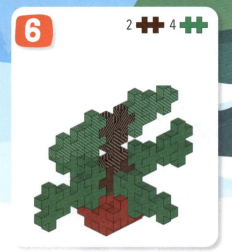

6   2 ✛   4 ✛

7   3 ✛

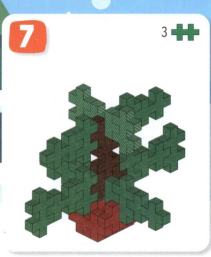

8   1 ✛

9 · 3

10 · 2

11 · 3 · 3

12 · 2

Decorate with stickers!

HOLLY JOLLY SANTA

1   1 ✚   1 ✚

2   2 ✚   5 ✚
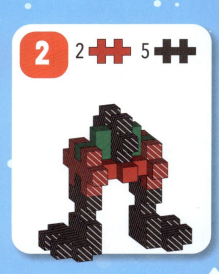

3   2 ✚

4   2 ✚   2 ✚

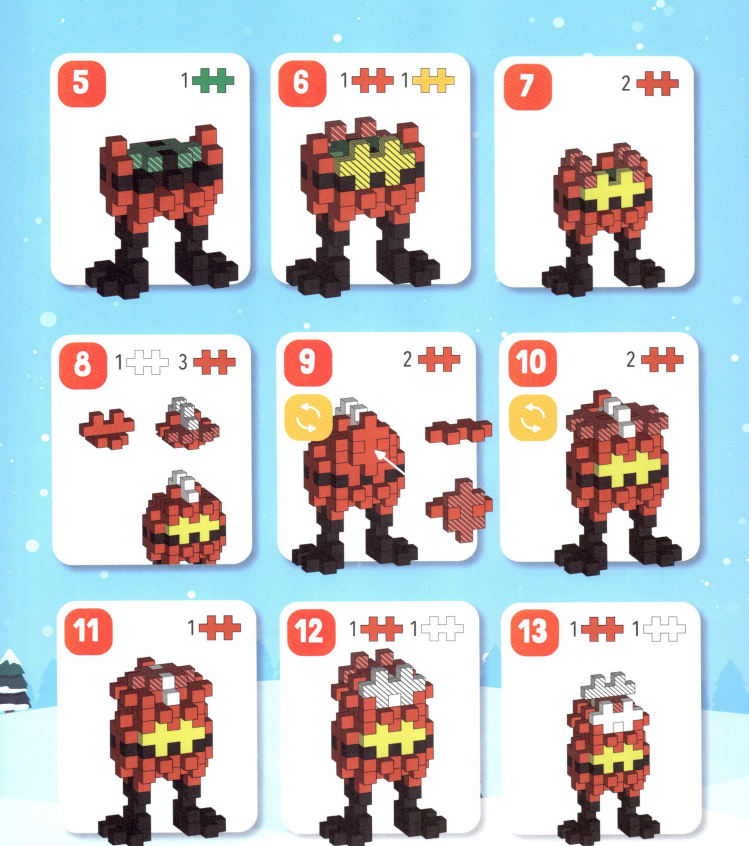

14 2

15 1

1
1
1

16 2

17 2

18 4

19 1

20 3

21 3

22 2

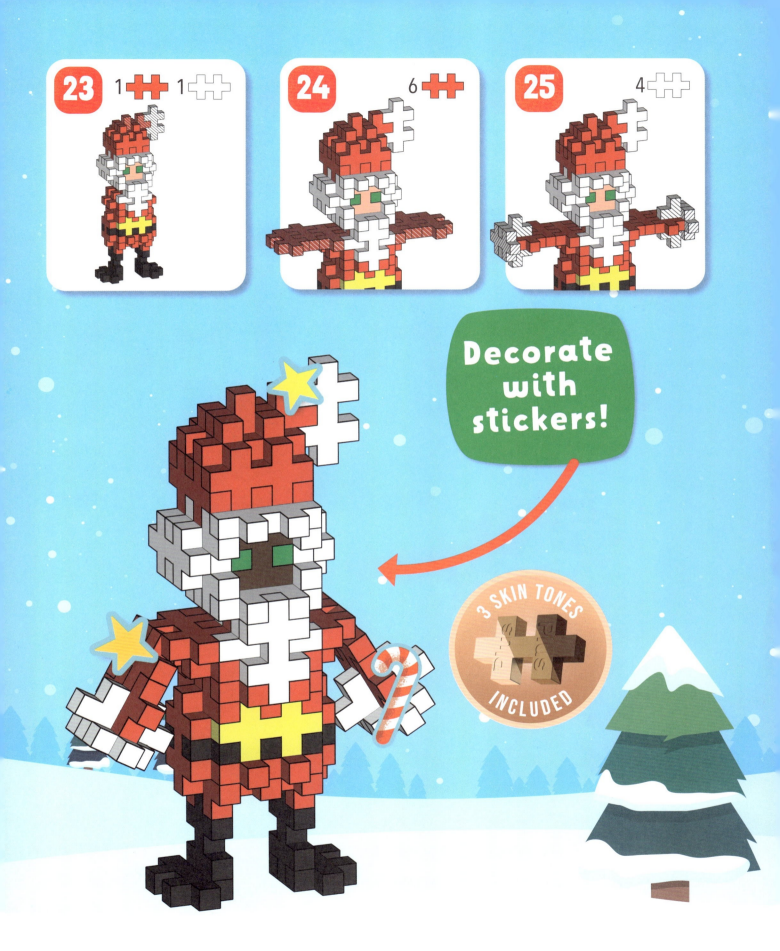

Decorate with stickers!

3 SKIN TONES INCLUDED

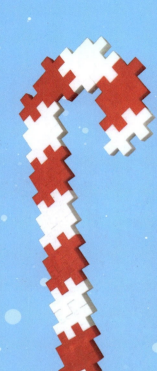

CANDY CANES

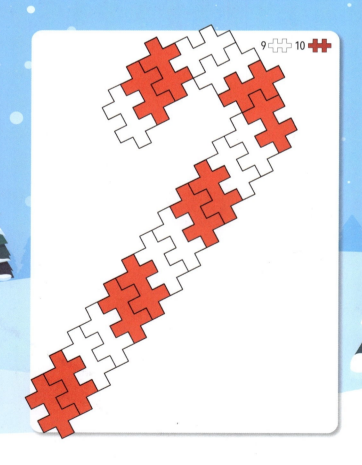